LORDSHIP

Danah I. Trammel

Fourth Printing
Copyright 1999 by Danah Trammel

ISBN - 0-9672108-0-1

Printed and bound in the U.S.A.

Unless otherwise indicated, all Scripture references are from the
Holy Bible: Authorized King James Version.
Other reference taken from Nelson's Illustrated Bible Dictionary,
Strong's concordance, Hebrew and Greek Lexicon

Other books by Danah Trammel:

Loosed from Binding the Devil
Declaring the Name of the Lord

WARNING

Satan and all his forces of darkness will fight against you, to keep you from reading this book. If while studying this book, and you notice unusual spiritual warfare, know that it is just a tactic of Satan to get you to put this book down.
DO NOT DO IT.
And if you do put it down, the forces of darkness will make sure you do not pick it back up again. Why???? Satan hates exposure, and the truth!! He is determined to keep you in bondage to the sin that is in your flesh, which he Lords over. It is time for his lordship to end, and the lordship of the true lord, Jesus Christ to begin. It is time for you to know the truth and let that truth <u>make</u> you free.
Free from sin and Satan's lordship.
Free to serve the true Lord, Jesus Christ.
Whom are you serving?
The Lord Jesus Christ, or the "god of this world, Satan".
It's time to know!

Your Lord (*Our Lord, through his Spirit, or Satan, through the flesh*) will expect his will to be served, his commands to be obeyed. and his desires fulfilled..

I thank God through Jesus Christ our Lord. So then with the mind I myself serve the law of God; but with the flesh the law of sin.
Romans 7:25

*Now the works of the flesh are manifest, which are these; Adultery, fornication, uncleanness, lasciviousness, Idolatry, witchcraft, hatred, variance, emulations, wrath, strife, seditions, heresies, Envyings, murders, drunkenness, revellings, and such like: of the which I tell you before, as I have also told you in time past, that they which do such **things shall not inherit the kingdom of God.***
Galatians 5:19-21

This is why Satan wants to keep you in bondage to your flesh!!
Your flesh disinherits *you* from the kingdom of God.
The kingdom of God is where all your blessings are!!
Satan knows if you stay under his lordship, you will not inherit the kingdom of God.

But the fruit of the Spirit is love, joy, peace, longsuffering, gentleness, goodness, faith, meekness, temperance: against such there is no law.
***And they that are Christ's have crucified the flesh with the affections and lusts.* .**
Galatians 5:22-24

When through the lordship of Jesus Christ, you allow him to crucify your flesh and you begin to walk after the SPIRIT, you will have a right to all the blessing contained in God's word.

That the righteousness of the law might be fulfilled in us, who walk not after the flesh, but after the Spirit.
Romans 8:4

As I stated before....**it is a matter of control.**
You will either be under the control of Satan through carnal man, or under the control of our Lord Jesus Christ through his HOLY SPIRIT.
If Jesus Christ is your Lord, you belong to Him, body, soul, and spirit.
As our Lord, he makes the decisions for our lives, we do not. Servants *serve!*

> *Know ye not, that to whom ye yield yourselves **servants to obey, his servants ye are** to whom ye obey; whether of sin unto death, or of obedience unto righteousness? Rom 6:16.*

Do not be deceived, you *are* someone's servant.
Whether of obedience to righteousness of Lord Jesus, or of unrighteousness to Satan.
Satan reigns through the carnal mind and fleshly lust.
Jesus Christ's reigns through the Holy Spirit.
If we concede to fleshly desires, to faithfully obey the flesh's affections and deceitful lusts, we are not celebrating the Lordship of Jesus Christ, but **opposing** it.
The flesh is vehemently **opposed** to God's government.

> *Because the carnal mind is enmity against God: for it is not subject to the law of God, **neither indeed can be** (Rom 8:7)*

Enmity _against_ God!
Enmity means "*AV-enemy, foe, a certain enemy*
*1) hated, odious, **hateful***
2) hostile, hating, and opposing another
  *2a) used of men as at enmity with God **by their sin***
    *2a1) **opposing (God) in the mind***
    2a2) a man that is hostile

A fleshly mind only wants what *it* wants. **It is against God!**
It will never be subject to God, **it cannot be.**

Satan is a master deceiver and a liar.
He deceives people into thinking that they can eventually bring
their flesh into subjection of Jesus Christ's lordship.
In the meantime, keep on doing what you want to do;
God's grace will be sufficient.

I do not frustrate the grace of God.
Galatians 2:21a
What shall we say then?
Shall we continue in sin, that grace may abound?
God forbid. *How shall we, that are dead to sin, live any longer therein?*
Rom 6:1

Do you know....

"WHO IS CONTROLLING YO?,
WHO IS REALLY YOUR MASTER???
WHOM DO YOU SERVE AND OBEY?
WHO DO YOU DISOBEY AND LET GO OF ??
Who is really your Lord?

Jesus Christ, the real Lord or Satan the God of this world.
As the scripture has said, "you cannot serve two masters,
you will cleave to one and let go of the other."
Whom do you cleave to??
Whom are you letting go of??
Again......It is time to know!!

Chapter Five

Lest Satan should get an advantage of us: for we are not ignorant of his <u>devices</u>.

2Co 2:11

Satan's Conspiracy

(It's an inside job)

Rom 7:15 For that which I do I allow not: for what I would, that do I not but what I hate, that do I.

Rom 7:16 If then I do that which I would not, I consent unto the law that [it is] good.

*Rom 7:17 Now then it is no more I that do it, but sin that dwelleth **in me**.*

*Rom 7:18 For I know that **in me (that is, in my flesh,)** dwelleth no good thing: for to will is present with me but how to perform that which is good I find not.*

Rom 7:19 For the good that I would I do not: but the evil which I would not, that I do.

*Rom 7:20 Now if I do that I would not, it is no more I that do it, but sin that dwelleth **in me**.*

Rom 7:21 I find then a law, that, when I would do good, evil is present with me.

Rom 7:22 For I delight in the law of God after the inward man:

Rom 7:23 But I see another law in my members, warring against the law of my mind, and bringing me into captivity to the law of sin which is in my members.

Rom 7:24 O wretched man that I am! who shall deliver me from the body of this death?

These scriptures speaks of a dilemma, that the *chief* Apostle, Apostle Paul was having with his flesh.
Look at verse 16-18, here Paul states
"the things he wants to do, **he does not do them**, and
the things he *hates,* **that he does!**"
Does this sound familiar?

should be doing he didn't do, and what he should
not be doing, he found himself doing!!
Paul concedes that it was no more him, but the "*sin that
dwelleth* (a inhabitation, any dwelling place, home) *in him*"
Paul the acknowledges that he found then a "law"

Greek – "*nomos*" 1) *anything established, a custom, a law, a command)*
a) law or rule producing a state b) thing that governs, controls or directs)

that was *warring* (*to oppose, war against*) in his members.
This "law" was the control of his old carnal man, his flesh.
The "*old man*", the carnal (fleshly) mind had *established*
control of our lives through lusts, desires and affections.

*That ye put off concerning the former conversation the old man,
which is corrupt according to the deceitful lusts; And have put on the
new man, which is renewed in knowledge after the image of him that
created him: Eph 4:22-23*

The "*old man*" was used to getting its way, doing its thing!
When the flesh commanded through its lusts and desires,
it was faithfully obeyed, (pleasure, drugs, sex, etc).
The self is only concerned with one thing, SELF!! It is selfish.
It is only concerned in getting what it wants.
Self is its own God. It has no regard God nor his will.
Self does not care about God or anyone else other than itself.
Self only wants to fulfill its own desires and its own will.
When you give Jesus Christ lordship of your life, he has to
"recreate" you through his Word, God's government.
(His Word, his will, his way).

*And that ye put on the new man, which after God is created
in righteousness and true holiness. Eph 4:24*

His new government establishes a new "law", a new way of
living, talking, and acting; which is totally opposite from the law
of sin that governed the old, fleshly-minded man.
That is when spiritual warfare begins.

*For the flesh lusteth against the Spirit, and the Spirit against the flesh:
and these are contrary the one to the other: so that ye cannot do the
things that ye would. Gal 5:17*

*But I see another law in my members, warring against the law of my
mind, and bringing me into captivity to the law of sin which is in my
members Rom 7:23*

Paul says the "law of sin" was his members (*not his church
members, he's speaking of his fleshly body and mind*!!),
was **warring** against the law of God (*in his mind*) and bringing
him back into captivity to the law of sin.

Interestingly enough, he states that this law that was fighting,
and battling him, was on the ***inside*** of him.

He delighted in the law of God (the Lordship of Jesus Christ)
after the inward man, but the law(control) of sin continued
"warring" against the law of God in his heart and mind.

Satan conspires with your "old man", to bring you <u>*back*</u> into
the captivity of the lusts of the flesh.

The law of sin keeps you carnally (*fleshly*) minded.

Satan knows that to be carnally minded is "death".

Death is separation.

Separation from the lordship of Jesus Christ in your life.

*For to be carnally minded **[is] death** but to be spiritually minded [is] life
and peace. Because the carnal mind[is] enmity against God:
for it is not subject to the law of God,neither indeed <u>can be</u>.
So then they that are in the flesh cannot please God.
Ro 8:6 - 8*

Satan knows that if you are carnally minded, that not only does
it separates you from God, but that you cannot please the very
one you say you praise and worship.

He conspires with the flesh (old lusts, habits, affections), stirs
them up to war against the lordship of the Lord Jesus Christ.

By using his demons in his servants, he causes trials,
tribulations, and aggravations, to stir up the works of the flesh,
(*anger, and bitterness, etc.*), to bring you back under the control
of the law of sin.
How?
The flesh does not like to suffer.
It likes to feel good. It likes everything it's way.
Comfortable, pleasurable, no hassle, no problems.
When the flesh has to give up its way, it balks, and begins to war
to get its way back.
Satan know that if the "old man", your flesh, begins to get its
way again, the lordship of Jesus Christ is over.
Satan then regains his lordship and the servant of the Lord
slowly backslides into SIN (the ways of the old man),
which results in: DEATH.

> *But every man is tempted, when he is drawn away of his own lust, and*
> *enticed.Then when lust hath conceived, it bringeth forth sin:*
> *and sin, when it is finished, bringeth forth death.*
> *James 1:14-15*
> *Forasmuch then as Christ hath suffered for us in the flesh, arm*
> *yourselves likewise with the same mind:*
> *for he that hath suffered in the flesh hath ceased from sin;*
> *1Peter 4:1*

You can allow Our Lord Jesus Christ to crucify you flesh,
which will cause it to suffer now, or you can allow Satan to
tempt with your flesh to open the door for sin which opens the
door for death and suffer eternally.

> *Likewise reckon ye also yourselves to be dead indeed into sin and alive*
> *to God through Jesus Christ our Lord.*
> *Rom 6:11*

Chapter Six

*Because the carnal mind is enmity against God: for it is not subject to the law of God, neither indeed **can be**. So then they that are in the flesh cannot please God.*

Romans 8:7-8

The "*carnal or fleshly mind, the old man* ", is God's enemy.
(Rom 8:7 says the "carnal mind" is "**enmity**"
(*odious, hateful, deep-seeded hatred*)
against God and is not subject to the law of God
(God's control or government),
NEITHER INDEED CAN BE!!
The "*carnal mind*" **can never** be subject to the Lordship
of Jesus Christ, therefore the Lordship of Jesus Christ
is out of the question for the carnally minded person.
The Greek word for "carnal" means - "*sarx*" - *flesh,
carnal, carnally minded, fleshly.*
1a) the sensuous nature of man, "the animal nature":
without any suggestion of depravity
the animal nature with cravings which incite to sin
2) a living creature (because possessed of a body of flesh)
whether man or beast.
3) the flesh, denotes **mere human nature, the earthly
nature of man apart from divine influence,
and therefore** *prone to sin* **and** *opposed to God.*
From these definitions, we can see the "*carnal*" mind
incites *(urge or encourage)* us to sin.
It is **by nature**, prone to sin and **opposed to God**.
The carnal mind or the Adamic nature of man cannot,
neither will not be subject to the Lordship of Jesus Christ.
It steadfastly opposes the control of the Holy Spirit,
and vice-versa (Gal 5:16).
Satan will continually fight to regain control through his
staunchest ally "*the carnal mind*".
If Satan can win the war in *your* members, to regain control,
he can get members of the body of Christ to resort back

to being "carnally minded", thereby giving him back
his authority, through sin, and putting him back in control!

For ye are yet carnal: for whereas [there is] among you envying, and
strife, and divisions, are ye not carnal, and walk as men? 1Co 3:3

That's why "the "old man" must be **crucified**".

Knowing this, that our old man is crucified with him, that the body of sin
might be destroyed, that henceforth we should not serve sin. Rom 6:6

Until the flesh is crucified, *__it will always be a battle for control__*.

But I see another law in my members,
warring against the law of my mind, and bringing me into captivity to
the law of sin which is in my members.
Rom 7:23

Knowing this, that our old man is crucified with him,
*that the body of sin **might be** destroyed,*
that henceforth we should not serve sin.
Rom 6:6

Satan wants you to *remain* his servants through the flesh.
In doing so, you deny Jesus Christ lordship, and end up where
Satan is going......**HELL**!!
It makes Satan no difference if you attend church faithfully,
sing in the choir, usher, etc., just **stay** carnally minded.
Satan retains Lordship over you regardless of how many
"hallelujahs" or "praise the Lord" comes out of your mouth.
What you say and what you do are two different things,

Be not deceived; God is not mocked:
for whatsoever a man soweth, that shall he also reap.
For he that soweth to his flesh shall of the flesh reap corruption;
but he that soweth to the Spirit shall of the Spirit reap life everlasting.
Gal 6:7-8

Chapter Seven

There is therefore now
no condemnation to them
which are in
Christ Jesus,
who walk not after the
flesh, but after the Spirit.

Romans 8:1

When we *initially* give Jesus Christ lordship we *were* carnally minded, but it's not God's will for us to *remain* carnally minded.

There is therefore now no condemnation to them which are in Christ Jesus, who walk not after the flesh, but after the Spirit.
Rom 8:1

This is why Rom 8:1 instructs us to *"WALK" after* the Spirit.

To *"walk"* means -, go, walk about, **be occupied**

1) to walk 1a) to make one's way, **progress**
2) to make due use of opportunities
3) to conduct one's self -3b) to pass one's life
4) the disposition or influence which **fills and governs** the soul

If we live in the Spirit, let us also walk in the Spirit.-
Gal 5:25

This I say therefore, and testify in the Lord, that ye henceforth walk not as other Gentiles walk, in the vanity of their mind,
Eph 4:17

Therefore to "walk after the Spirit" means to:
PROGRESSIVELY begin to be controlled, influenced and governed by God through the Lordship (government) of Jesus Christ, our Lord, through the power of the Holy Ghost.

"Be Filled with the Spirit(Holy Ghost)"...Gal 5:18
(To influenced or governed by the Holy Spirit)
That ye might be filled with the knowledge of his will in all wisdom and spiritual understanding...Col 1:9
Being filled with the fruits of righteousness, which are by Jesus Christ, unto the glory and praise of God. Phil 1:11

Therefore, you progressively go from being controlled by Satan through your flesh, the carnal man, to being controlled by our Lord Jesus, through the Holy Spirit.

One step at a time, it will not happen all at once.

God's righteousness is fulfilled in those who walk **NOT** after the flesh (carnal mind) but after the Spirit. *(Rom 8:4)*

In order to "walk not after the flesh" we must have a renewed mind and a new will.

Satan does not want you to make a progressive movement in the Lord, AND you can't stay in one place, you will either progress or regress (backslide)

Please note - GOD IS NOT married to the backslider... he was married to Israel and _Isreal_ was backsliding.

*Go and proclaim these words toward the north, and say, Return, thou **backsliding Israel**, saith the LORD; and I will not cause mine anger to fall upon you: for I am merciful, saith the LORD, and I will not keep anger for ever.Turn, O backsliding children, saith the LORD; for I am married unto you: Jer 3:12 &14a*

We must be taught how to "walk after the Spirit" by the Spirit of God, and stop walking after the flesh.

That the righteousness of the law might be fulfilled in us, who walk not after the flesh, but after the Spirit.

Rom 8:4

We progressively walk away from obeying the lust of our flesh to obeying the will of God.

One does not instantaneously go from being carnal minded to being spiritually mind, it is a process.

That process can only be completed by the Lord Jesus Christ, through his Holy Spirit.

This I say then, Walk in the Spirit, and ye shall not fulfil the lust of the flesh.

Gal 5:16

This is why we must "*walk* the walk", not "*talk* the walk"

Our walk must change.

We cannot walk after the Spirit of God and continue to fulfill the lust of the flesh.

In order to walk after the Spirit, the flesh with its lust and affections, the enmity against God, must be crucified.

It will not die on its own. It must be crucified.

We will not crucify our own flesh, only through the lordship of the Lord Jesus Christ is he able to crucify the flesh.

> *And they that are Christ's have crucified the flesh*
> *with the affections and lusts.*
> *Gal 5:24*
> *This I say therefore, and testify in the Lord, that ye henceforth **walk not** as other Gentiles walk, in the vanity of their mind,*
> *Having the understanding darkened, being alienated from the life of God through the ignorance that is in them, because of the blindness of their heart:*
> *Who being past feeling have given themselves over unto lasciviousness, to work all uncleanness with greediness.*
> *But ye have not so learned Christ;*
> *If so be that ye have heard him, and **have been taught by him**, as the truth is in Jesus: That ye put off concerning the former conversation the old man, **which is corrupt according to the deceitful lusts**;*
> *And be renewed in the spirit of your mind; and **that ye put on the new man, which after God is created in righteousness and true holiness.***
> *Eph 4:17-24*

These scriptures say it all.

Our walk has to, and will change.

Henceforth, after we give the Lord Jesus Christ lordship of our life, we will no longer walk like we used to.

Our Lord wants to makes us new, **after** he crucifies the flesh.

Notice it says "*the new man*", which is **created** in righteousness and true holiness (not a religion).

> *Furthermore then we beseech you, brethren, and exhort you by the Lord Jesus, that as ye have received of us how **ye ought to walk and to please God**, so ye would abound more and more.*
> *For God hath not called us unto uncleanness, but unto holiness*
> *1 Thess 4:1 &7a*
> *For ye were sometimes darkness, but now are ye light in the Lord: walk as children of light: Eph 5:8*

Know ye not that the unrighteous shall not inherit the kingdom of God?
Be not deceived: neither fornicators, nor idolaters, nor adulterers,
nor effeminate, nor abusers of themselves with mankind,
Nor thieves, nor covetous, nor drunkards, nor revilers, nor
extortioners, shall inherit the kingdom of God. And such were some
of you: but ye are washed, but ye are sanctified, but ye are justified in
the name of the Lord Jesus, and by the Spirit of our God.
1 Cor 6:9-11

A change in "our walk" is very important, and vital.

Will you stumble or fall, sometimes?

Of course you will, but if you do, you will not be under condemnation, because you are no longer walking after the flesh, but after the Spirit.

God's grace will cover your stumbling.

And he said unto me, My grace is sufficient for thee: for my strength is
made perfect in weakness. 2Co 12:9 a

Is grace an excuse to keep sinning (walking after your fleshly lusts)?

What shall we say then? Shall we continue in sin, that grace may
abound? **God forbid.**
How shall we, that are dead to sin, live any longer therein?
Rom 6:1-2
For sin shall not have dominion over you: for ye are not under the law,
but under grace.
Ro 6:14
What then? shall we sin, because we are not under the law, but under
grace? **God forbid.**
Ro 6:15
If we say that we have fellowship with him,
and walk in darkness, we lie, and do not the truth:
1Jo 1:6

Our new walk becomes a progressive movement.
Not standing still, but constantly moving towards our new Lord
(Jesus Christ) and his government of righteousness and away
from our old Lord (Satan) and his government of sin.
Our Lord Jesus Christ will teach you how to walk after him.
It will require total obedience to the lordship of Jesus Christ.
It will involve prayer, studying his Word, seeking his will and
adapting to his way.
Allowing him to re-create you into a new creature.
It is a process.
The process begins with your walk.....one step at a time.
How you walk determines not only lordship,
but the direction in which you are going.
Up or down.

Chapter Eight

Nevertheless the
foundation of God
standeth sure, having this
seal, The Lord knoweth
them that are his.
And, let every one that
nameth the name of Christ
depart from iniquity

2 Timothy 2:19

What Jesus will say to those who never gave him Lordship?
"Depart from me ye that work iniquity.."
The Greek word for "iniquity" is *"anomia"*, *unrighteousness,*
transgression of the law the condition of without law
a) <u>contempt and violation of law,</u> *iniquity,* **wickedness**
b) **without law**, *transgressor, wicked, lawless* <u>destitute of God's law</u>
c) <u>**not subject to the law or the government of our Lord Jesus Christ**</u>
Therefore "iniquity" is doing what one wants to do, regardless of
God's law (his word), *KNOWING* it's sin and doing it anyway,
(*contempt and violation of God's law*) not desiring or allowing
God's government in one's life (*destitute of God's law*).
Lawless (not willing to be governed) nor being subject to the
government of the Lord Jesus, (his lordship),
To live under the control the carnal mind will cause one to
work iniquity, because the flesh is not subject to the law
(or government) of God, neither indeed can be!
Going to church every Sunday, and living an iniquitous life
Monday through Saturday is Satan's agenda.
Do what you want to do, what you are big enough to do!
And isn't it a crock that some will party in Satan's nightclub
on Saturday night, then Sunday morning, walk proudly into
God's house, thinking that going to church will make everything
right!?!?!
Please do not equate church going with salvation.
That is one of Satan's most deceptive tactic.
Going to church does "unmake" you a worker of iniquity!
Even so ye also outwardly appear righteous unto men,
but within ye are full of hypocrisy and iniquity. Mt 23:28
When one continues to do what they want to do, without
regard of God's word or his will, they work (*to do, exercise,*
perform, commit, produce) iniquity.

Yes, Satan loves for Christians to "**look**" holy.

Because it is written, Be ye holy; for I am holy. 1Pe 1:16

Satan has deceived many into thinking that just because
they attend church every Sunday they are alright with God.
"Look the look", "talk the talk", just don't "walk the walk".

The Son of man shall send forth his angels,
and they shall gather out of his kingdom all things
***that offend, and them which do iniquity** Mt 13:41*

Iniquity is a very serious offense in the eyesight of God.
What does the word of God says about iniquity....

And the tongue [is] a fire, a world of iniquity: Jas 3:6

Are the words you speak God's word or words of iniquity...
..... gossiping, backbiting, cursing, lying, etc? If so, "iniquity"

I speak after the manner of men because of the infirmity of your flesh:
for as ye have yielded your members servants to uncleanness and to
iniquity unto iniquity even so now yield your members servants to
righteousness Rom 6:19

Do you secretly do evil things to those you don't care for
or to those who have wronged you? If so, iniquity!

because iniquity abound, the love of many shall wax cold." Mt 24:12

Truly the love of God has waxed so cold, in the body of Christ.
There is hardly any love in the body of Christ.
Many would rather see you fall than help you up.
Many say they have the love of God, but close up their
bowels of compassion to brethren in need.
Because of iniquity God's love cannot flow.

***Woe** to them that devise **iniquity**, and work evil upon their beds!*
when the morning is light, they practice it,
because it is in the power of their hand.
Mic 2:1

The way of the LORD [is] strength to the upright: but destruction shall
be to the workers of iniquity
Pr 10:29

*If I regard iniquity in my heart, **the Lord will not hear [me]: Ps 66:18***
*The foolish shall not stand in thy sight: **thou hatest** all workers of*
iniquity. Ps 5:5

These are just a few of the scriptures on iniquity.

There are 262 scriptures in God's word on iniquity.

GOD HATES INIQUITY, and the "workers of iniquity" are those who do iniquity.

A "worker of iniquity" is "lawless, without control", and has no regard for authority or government in their life.

They break God's and man's laws with reckless disregard.

They want their way and if they can not get what they want, they devise evil ways to have it, regardless of who gets hurt, used or abused.

Nevertheless the foundation of God standeth sure, having this seal,
The Lord knoweth them that are his. And, Let every one
that nameth the name of Christ depart from iniquity. 1 Tim 2:19

The Word of God says to **"depart** *(to make stand off, cause to withdraw, to remove, to revolt, to desert, withdraw from)*
from iniquity".

To desert, withdraw from or revolt from Satan

He will bring on the spiritual warfare, pull out all the top guns… (lusts, affections, etc) to get you back!

But he is a defeated foe!

Satan hates it when you revolt against him, that is why he wants you to *revolt against* God with your iniquity!

Turn the revolt around….flip the script!!!

Revolt against Satan by departing from iniquity, and please God by giving our Lord Jesus, lordship of your life!

You can only do that through the lordship of Jesus

Be not deceived, it will definitely take the Lordship of Jesus Christ for one to depart from iniquity.

Chapter Nine

The Lord knoweth how to deliver the godly out of temptations, and to reserve the unjust unto the day of judgment to be punished:

2Pe 2:9

Back To "That Day"

SO THEN, ON "*THAT DAY*"
WHAT WILL IT BE?????
WILL THERE BE REJOICING,?
OR WEEPING AND GNASHING OF THE TEETH??

WHAT WILL OUR LORD JESUS SAY TO YOU?

"DEPART FROM ME, I NEVER KNEW YOU"!
or
"WELL DONE THOU GOOD AND FAITHFUL SERVANT"

My friend, it is either Heaven or the lake of fire (through Hell),
there are no alternatives.

And if thy right hand offend thee, cut it off, and cast it from thee: for it is
profitable for thee that one of thy members should perish, and not that
thy whole body should be cast into hell.
Mt 5:30
And the sea gave up the dead which were in it; and death and hell
delivered up the dead which were in them: and they were judged
every man according to their works.
And death and hell were cast into the lake of fire.
This is the second death.
And whosoever was not found written in the book of life
was cast into the lake of fire.
Rev 20:13-15
And I saw the dead, small and great, stand before God; and the books
were opened: and another book was opened, which is the book of life:
and the dead were judged out of those things which
were written in the books, according to their works.
Rev 20:12

So it is Heaven or Hell. The choice is yours.
If our Lord Jesus says "depart from me," please think about it,
where you're going??!!
Beloved, heaven and hell is very real.
If you desire permanent residence in Heaven, you must put off
corruptible and put on incorruptible.
It is only possible through the lordship of Jesus Christ.

And why call ye me, Lord, Lord, and do not the things which I
say?
Luke 6:46
Don't just call Jesus Lord, give him LORDSHIP!

PLEASE do not take a chance with the only soul you have.
After you leave this earth, there will be no second chances.
You have a chance now, to get it right and keep it right.
That is why our Lord Jesus sacrificed his life.
Whom God hath set forth to be a propitiation through faith in his blood,
to declare his righteousness for the remission of sins that are past,
through the forbearance of God;
Ro 3:25
And he is the propitiation for our sins: and not for ours only, but also for
the sins of the whole world.
1Jo 2:2
Herein is love, not that we loved God, but that he loved us, and sent his
Son to be the propitiation for our sins.
1Jo 4:10

If you're not sure, and you want to get it right with our Lord
Jesus Christ by giving him lordship of your life,
Pray this prayer now.....-
"Lord Jesus, I confess my sins and iniquities,
I repent of them and ask you to forgive me. I am truly sorry.
I believe that you died on the cross for my sins,
And that you paid my sins debt.
I truly believe in my heart that God raised you from the dead
and that you are both LORD and CHRIST.
Lord Jesus, I give you (or give you back!!) "lordship"
of my life today. I yield to your control of my life.
I am willing for you to lord over me and I trust in your Lordship.
I believe, that by faith, I have received forgiveness, and
I believe that I have been accepted into your kingdom.
By faith, I now receive the gift of the Holy Ghost that will
empower me to be conformed into your image.
Thank You Lord Jesus, for saving me.
I accept your control of my life
I am your servant. Use me Lord to bring you glory
Satan, you will no longer Lord over me through my flesh.
You are not my lord anymore,
Jesus Christ is my new lord and him only will I serve."
Amen

Jesus Christ is now your Lord and you have given him the
right to exercise his lordship over you.
Our Lord is a good Lord, so do not be fearful of the where he
will lead you.

The steps of a good man are <u>ordered</u> by the LORD:
and he delighteth in his way. , Ps 37:23

Yes, you life will change.

Yes, Satan will war against you to regain his lordship.

But now you will no longer be the victim, but the VICTOR.

Now thanks be unto God, which always causeth us to triumph in Christ,
2Co 2:14

And please, do not refer to your lord as just "Jesus" anymore.

He is **Jesus Christ _your_ Lord or your Lord Jesus Christ**.

In celebrating our Lord, we don't refer to our Lord Jesus as just "Jesus", we would then be robbing Him of His God-given deity according to Acts 2:36. (Please read my lastest book -
Declaring the Name of the Lord)

Allow our Lord Jesus Christ to have his way in your life.

Yes, he **must** crucify your flesh, but he knows how to do it.

Remember if our Lord Jesus Christ is not Lord **of all**;

he is not Lord **at all**!!

Yes, your flesh will suffer, and want to return to it ld way of life, that is why it's very important to declare, agree and concede that Jesus Christ is your Lord **daily**.

What next?

1. Pray daily. Ask our Lord to bless you with a prayer partner.
2. Declare that Jesus Christ as your Lord in every situation, allow him to Lord over you and the situation.
   That is why it is important to study his word so you may know how to govern yourself according to his word.
3. Allow our Lord Jesus to control you, emotionally, spiritually, and physically.
4. Be willing for our Lord to crucify your flesh with it's affections and lusts.
5. STUDY your Lord's word to learn more about him.
6. Fellowship with like-minded believers.

God Bless You!
You have made the best decision you could have ever made.
Remember, it's a process, it will take time.
Let patience have her perfect(*ing*) work.
And may God our Father continue to enrich and enlighten your Spirit.

Jesus Christ is **both** Lord and Christ.
To him be Praise, and Honor, and Power and Glory.
Amen.

About the Author

Prophet Danah Trammel has been in the ministry since 1980, as an Prophetess, Teacher, Evangelist, Pastor, and Christian Counselor. Prophet Trammel was ordained as an Evangelist and Pastor by the House of God Prayer For All People Ministries, in Philadelphia, PA Prophet Trammel is currently Pastor of The Lord's Tabernacle, located in Winder and Stone Mountain, GA.

Prophet Trammel earned her Associates of Arts degree in Theology at the Grace Christian College, formerly located in E. Point, GA., and received her Bachelor of Theology in Religious Studies in September, 2004.

Traveling extensively around the United States and soon abroad, Prophet Trammel's ministry assignment in life is to teach God's people the Lordship of our Lord Jesus and the kingdom principles that embodies his Lordship"; through "Lordship" conferences.

"Jesus our Lord is the King", we are his body, we have a an inherited right to the Kingdom of God and all the blessings contained therein". Equipping God's people with the authority and power to retain their kingdom rights, Prophet Trammel, also conducts an informative, yet powerful Spiritual Warfare conference.

Believing that the "anointing destroys the yoke", and that it is God's will for his people to be free from the law of "sin and death", Prophet Trammel teaches the principle of God's word, and then allows the delivering power of the Holy Ghost to flow through her to destroy the yokes of bondage that have God's people in bondage..

These conferences enriches, empowers and revives the body of Christ. For conference bookings, please call **404-348-4086**.

To reorder this or any of the other books, call the telephone number above or visit our website **www.Thelordstabernacle.com**

Prophet Trammel solicits your continued prayers.

ORDER FORM

Name _____

Address_____

City, State, Zip _____

Telephone number _____

Please send me the following book(s): (*Postage paid*)

_____ LORDSHIP ($7.95)
_____ DECLARING THE NAME OF THE LORD ($9.95)
_____ LOOSED FROM BINDING THE DEVIL ($6.95)

I HAVE ENCLOSED $_____ FOR PAYMENT OF
THESE BOOKS.

Mail to: The Kingdom Press
P. O. Box 1718
Winder, GA. 30680
Or
Fax to: 404-348-4086 x103

*Coming soon, you will be able to can download LORDSHIP
in an ebook. Check our website for more details.*

CB Dedications CB

This book is dedicated to all of the blessings God has put in my life and in the Ministry..

To my church family of The Lord's Tabernacle, past and present, you have truly taught me what lordship is all about, and I praise our Lord Jesus Christ for you all.

To my precious prayer group, your prayers and intercession mean so much. You all are such a blessing, and I thank Our Lord Jesus Christ for you all.

Apostle Larry and Prophet Machele Bardge, your support, insight, revelation and spiritual guidance is such a blessing.

Pastor Sarah Harper and Evangelist Elizabeth Heath, you guys taught me the value of prayer, for which I will always be grateful.

Apostle Catherine Whitaker, thank you for your inspiration throughout the years.

My children…..Tink and Chanique

Nannah's babies…. Cymberli, Joshua, Elijah, Amber, Makalah, and Trinity.

To every ministry who opened a door of ministry to me to teach this Apostolic word to the Body of Christ.

To every Saint of God that has encouraged, discouraged, loved, hated, lifted me up, put me down.

It has all worked for my good.

And a special "thank you" to Brother Ellis Sullivan. ☺

May Jehovah God our Heavenly Father, continue to richly bless you all, through our blessed Lord Jesus Christ.

Forward

Throughout time, the controversy over the Lordship of
Jesus Christ has sparked heated debates, arguments,
and biblical philosophical studies among some of
the greatest Bible scholars.
It has and still causes a great divide in the body of Christ,
the doctrine of Grace vs Lordship!!
The reason for this divide is because "lordship" is NOT a
doctrine, it is a way of life. A life Satan does want the Body of
Christ to live. That's why he is vehemently opposed to the
Lordship of the Lord Jesus Christ.
Before our Lord Jesus began to deal with me about Lordship,
quite frankly I had never even heard of "Lordship".
I am sure that this may be the case with many.
Just what is lordship? And what does it have to do with
salvation? Well let me share my testimony with you.
My Testimony……..
One day while I was in my prayer closet, making strong
petitions to the Lord, and calling upon the Lord, fervently!!
After making my petitions known, The Lord Jesus Christ spoke
something so profound it scared me; he said
"I'm not your Lord!" "What!! The devil is a lie!! I said
I've been saved for 15 years; I lived what I though was a saved
life, a life pleasing to the Lord Jesus Christ.
I thought sure that I was "all that" in the Lord.
The Lord Jesus Christ used me to prophesy, heal and minister to
his people all over the U.S. People were saved, delivered and
blessed through the ministry.
So naturally I was deeply concerned when he spoke this to me.

How could the Lord Jesus Christ say that to me ???
Thinking, "this is just the devil", I left the prayer closet.
Well, the next day I went back into my prayer closet, and
The Lord Jesus Christ spoke the same thing. **"I'm not your
Lord!** You do *what* you want to do, *when* you want to do it,
and *with whom* you want to do it with, that is not lordship".
Okay, now this really startled me!
I replied "Lord, I have never even heard of lordship!"
He replied "study it". I knew then that this was the
Lord Jesus Christ speaking to me.
The enemy wanted me to believe that it a demon talking to me,
but it was not; it was our Lord Jesus Christ.
So I looked up the word "lordship" in the Bible, and there were
2 scriptures; Matt10:42 and Luke 22:25, but neither passage
referred to the Lord Jesus Christ.
Puzzled, I went back to the Lord, and again he instructed me to
study "lordship" and principles that embodies lordship.
He then instructed me to write a book and teach his Church
about his lordship.
With no prior knowledge about "lordship", I have researched
God's word, lexicons, concordances, and through the leading,
training and guidance of the Holy Ghost, I have wrote this
Apostolic message, which was sent from our Lord Jesus Christ
to his Body, the Church.
What our Lord Jesus Christ has led me to write in this book,
is not just a theory or a doctrine, it is a way of life.
Every since our Lord Jesus Christ revealed "lordship" to me,
I have been endeavoring, every day, to allow him to *be* my Lord.
I have seen this message change many lives.
It has certainly changed my life.
I'm sure it will change yours too.

Table of Contents

Chapter One
That day!

And I saw a great white throne, and him that
sat on it, from whose face the earth and the
heaven fled away;
and there was found no place for them.
And I saw the dead, small and great, stand
before God; and the books were opened: and
another book was opened, which is the book of
life: and the dead were judged out of those
things which were written in the books,
according to their works.

Re 20:11-12

sing
along

"When we all get to
Heaven, what a day of rejoicing
that will beeeee.....
When we alllllll see Jesus, we will
sing and shout the Victoorryyy"

NOT!
WHY NOT?

Not every one that <u>saith</u> unto me,
Lord, Lord, shall enter into the kingdom of heaven...
<u>*Many*</u> *will say to me in that day,*
Lord, Lord, have we not prophesied in thy name? And in
thy name have cast out devils? And in thy name done
many wonderful works?
And then will I profess unto them,
<u>**I never knew you**</u>:**depart from me,**
ye that work iniquity.
Matthew 7:21-24

8

I've got good new, and I've got bad news.

The "good news" is that everybody is going to Heaven!!!!

That's right, everybody! No matter what they have done in life.

The "bad news" is everybody will not stay.

Everyone will stand before the great white throne of judgment.

And, the great white throne of judgment is *very* real.

When I first got saved, our Lord gave me an out of body
experience and took me to Heaven and showed me the great
white throne of judgment.

When we get to heaven!! What a glorious day!

When we go to be with the Lord!! It will be worth it all!

Christians sing about "that glorious day" all the time.

With euphoric anticipation, we envision our arrival into
Heaven. Oh yes, when we get to Heaven........

We vividly imagine how we're going to put on our long white
robes and dance around Heaven all day; telling all our friends
and love ones "Howdy, howdy!" and so on, and so on.

For some, it *will* be a glorious day, however, according to
Matt 7:23-24, for others, it will be a sad and dreadful day.

Many will sound their spiritual and religious accolades,
about what they did and how well they did it.

Many will say to me in that day, Lord, Lord, have we not prophesied in
thy name? and in thy name have cast out devils? and in thy name done
many wonderful works? Matt 7:22

Many will stand before our Lord Jesus with expectation of
hearing *"well done, thou good and faithful servant,"*
only to hear:

And then will I profess unto them, I never knew you:
depart from me, ye that work iniquity. Matt 7:23

If you must depart from the Lord Jesus Christ, there is only one
other place you can go!!

What kind of day will it be for you? What will you hear?
Will one's genealogy, education, social or economical status
account for anything? *Sorry, no it won't*
How about one's dynamic singing or preaching ability? *Uh-huh*
Maybe one's position or title in the church? *Nope*
What about church affiliation? (*Baptist, Holiness, etc*) *Nope!*
What will matter then? What will be the determining factor?
Who will be saved? According to the word of God…..

> That if thou shalt <u>confess with thy mouth the Lord Jesus</u>, and shalt
> <u>***believe in thine heart***</u> that God hath raised him from the dead,
> thou **shalt** be saved. Rom 10:10

Many will say, "Oh I have confessed Jesus as Lord", however,
your confession of our Lord Jesus Christ is just the *beginning*
of the process of salvation.
It will take the lordship of Jesus Christ to complete the work of
salvation in your life, because salvation *is* a process.
Oh yes, you may *call* Jesus "Lord", and may have confessed
Jesus him as your Lord and Savior, but is Jesus Christ *really*
Lord? You may believe that he is Lord, but giving him
Lordship is an entirely different matter.
We can "call" him Lord all we want to, but are we allowing
Jesus Christ to *be* our Lord??
Do you know *how* to allow the Lord Jesus to lord over you?
Or are you relying on false hopes and promises, such as religion,
observing religious traditions or religious affiliation?

Who is really *your* LORD?
<u>*Jesus Christ the true and risen Lord*</u>
<u>*or Satan the God of this world*</u>
It is time to know!!

Chapter Two

Jesus Christ is Lord!

"Therefore let all the house
of Israel
know assuredly,
that God
hath made that same Jesus,
whom ye have crucified,
both
Lord and Christ."

Acts: 2:36

Jesus Christ is Lord, and our Lord Jesus is the Christ.

God made him **both** Lord and Christ.

Not one or the other....BOTH.

As Christ he delivered you from the penalty of sin, by paying for your sins with his own blood.

As Lord, he keeps you from sinning by delivering you from the power of sin, contained in the body of sin, thereby giving you the victory over sin.

But he must have "lordship" as a Lord, to deliver you.

When you "received" Jesus Christ, did that make him your Lord?

Do you know what it means to *allow* the Lord Jesus Christ to *be* Lord of your life, *everyday*, not just on Sunday?

Who has total control of your ways, your actions, and your will?

Who makes the decisions regarding your life?

Who you decides what is best for you?

Or do you depend upon extenuating factors in your life such as your education, political or social affiliations, your job, or your genealogy to decide how you should or should not live?

Who made the decision of how you would live your life?

We are taught very early in life to set career goals for our life.

Did you consult the Lord Jesus Christ when you set those goals?

Or were those goals a fulfillment of a childhood desire?

Or did your parents plan and direct your destiny?

When we plan our own destinies we are in direct violation of God's word.

The steps of a good man are ordered by the LORD:
and he delighteth in his way Ps 37:23
For I know the thoughts that I think toward you, saith the LORD,
thoughts of peace, and not of evil, to give you an expected end.
Jer 29:11

Only the Lord Jesus Christ knows what is best for us.

There is a way which seemeth right unto a man,
but the end thereof are the ways of death.
Pr 14:12

God made Jesus both Christ and Lord for a purpose.
First to redeem you then to ensure your redemption.
Even though God made him Lord of all (*Matt 28:18*),
only you can make him *your* Lord, by giving him Lordship.
Only you can actually allow him to *be* your Lord.
When you do what you want to do or whatever is convenient for
you, you are *not* allowing the Lord Jesus Christ to lord over you,
even though you are calling him "Lord".
Many times Jesus Christ is called "lord" but not allowed
to be Lord, nor fulfill his Kingly position in our lives.
This is due mainly because our "carnal man, our flesh wants to
do, *what* it wants to, *when* it want to and with *whom* it wants
to do it with.
Flesh wants what it wants.
It hates to be disciplined or corrected.
Flesh does not like to be told what to do, nor be controlled,
let alone lorded over.

" And say not, Who shall control me for my works?
*for the Lord will surely revenge thy pride". **Sirach 5: 3***

Flesh wants to be in control , that is until trouble.
Then we want the Lord Jesus Christ to step in and get us out of
the trouble our flesh gets us into, and we want him to do it in a
hurry!
We expect for the Lord Jesus Christ to keep the promises
contained in his Word, keep us safe, bless us, prosper us,
just let us live the way we want to live.

We want the Lord Jesus Christ to keep his word, so as Lord he want us to keep his Word too.

But he said, Yea rather, blessed are they that hear the word of God, and keep it. Lu 11:28

When a situation or circumstance that is not favorable or conducive to the flesh's liking, or how the flesh planned it, the flesh takes control by doing what it want to do and not what the Word of God says to do.

When this happens, we are not allowing Jesus Christ to be Lord. Jesus Christ is the Word of God. (*John 1: 1-3*)

If we are not submissive to the Word of God, we are not submissive to the Lordship of Jesus Christ.

Submissiveness to the Lordship of Jesus Christ must be taught, defined and clarified on a daily basis.

A "Christian" is a disciple of the Lord Jesus Christ.

A disciple is a learner, or pupil.

And the disciples were called Christians first in Antioch. Acts 11:26

We must be taught God's Word, God's will and God's way.

As Lord, Jesus Christ teaches us God's Word, God's way, and God's will. He then renews our minds, empowers us to "put on" the new man, which is created after righteousness and true holiness, all the while crucifying the very one that hates to be taught or disciplined; our flesh.

And that ye put on the new man, which after God is created in righteousness and true holiness. Eph 4:24

But Jesus Christ must **be** Lord to do this.

That is why the flesh rebels against the lordship of Jesus Christ. If the flesh gets its way, you can *call* Jesus Christ "lord" all you want to, but he will not *be* Lord.

When it comes to discipline and correction, true Lordship is then challenged, determined and clarified!

Sadly, many are deceived into believing that adhering to
religious doctrines or traditions is a substitute for salvation.
It is not. Nor is it a substitute for lordship.
Sin is disobedience to God (*his Word, his Will, his Way*).
There is no justification for sin not matter how sincere one is.

*"For the wages of sin **is death**; but the gift of God is eternal life through
Jesus Christ our Lord." Rom 6:23. "*

As Christ, Jesus paid for our sins once and for all.
As Lord, he delivers us from the power of Sin lording over us
as it did before we gave Jesus Christ lordship.
But what about Grace, after all we are under Grace, right?

*"What shall we say then? Shall we
continue in sin, that grace may abound? God forbid.
How shall we, that are dead to sin, live any longer therein?*
Romans 6:1-2

So what can we do? Nobody is perfect right?

*O wretched man that I am! who shall deliver me from the body of this
death? I thank God through Jesus Christ our Lord.
So then with the mind I myself serve the law of God;
but with the flesh the law of sin.*
Rom 7:24-25

That is why Jesus Christ has to be your Lord.
Only by his Power and authority over sin; can he deliver
you from the power of sin.

*For if we have been planted together in the likeness of his death, we
shall be also in the likeness of his resurrection:
Knowing this, that our old man is crucified with him, that the body of sin
might be destroyed, that henceforth we should not serve sin.*
Rom 6:5-6

You will either serve the Lord Jesus Christ or sin.
One of them *will* lord over you.
You make the decision which.
If you don't make the decision, your flesh will make it for you.

God's Word declares the Lordship of Jesus Christ

Acts 2:36 *Let all the house of Israel know assuredly that God hath made that same Jesus, whom ye have crucified,* **both LORD and Christ.**

Col 2:6 *As ye have therefore* <u>received</u> **Christ Jesus the Lord,** *[so] walk ye in him:*

Ro 5:1 *Therefore being justified by faith, we have peace with God through* **our Lord Jesus Christ:**

Ro 6:11 *Likewise reckon ye also yourselves to be dead indeed unto sin, but alive unto God through Jesus Christ our Lord.*

Ro 5:11 *And not only so, but we also joy in God through our Lord Jesus Christ, by whom we have now received the atonement.*

1Co 15:57 *But thanks be to God, which giveth us the victory through our Lord Jesus Christ*

Ro 16:18 *For they that are such* **serve not our Lord Jesus Christ,** *but their own belly and by good words and fair speeches deceive the hearts of the simple.*

We serve God by obeying his Word and doing his Will, our Lord Jesus Christ *is* the Word of God.

> *And the Word was made flesh, and dwelt among us,*
> *(and we beheld his glory, the glory as of the only begotten*
> *of the Father,) full of grace and truth. John 1:14*

We serve Sin by obeying Satan's will.
It is up to you *whom* you serve.

What is a Lord, anyway ??

Lord. Webster's Thesaurus defines a "Lord" as -
a leader, chief, commander, a king, a master, a governor, monarch or potentate.
To Greek and Hebrew definitions for *"Lord"* is
Greek - *"kurios"* meaning. "supremacy".
It also means *"Lord, master .*
a) he to whom a person or thing *"belongs"*, about which
   he, *(the lord)* has the power of deciding master, lord
b) the possessor and disposer of a thing, **the owner,**
   the one who has *control of the person*, the master
c) is a title of honor expressive of respect and reverence,
   with which *servants salute their master*
d) this title is given to Jesus Christ, the Messiah
The Greek word "kurios" is taken from the root word
"kuriakos" {koo-ree-ak-os'}, meaning *"belonging to the Lord"*
The Lord who has dominion over , exercises lordship over,
is Lord of *to be lord of,* to rule, *have dominion over to exercise*
influence upon, **to have power over,** *government, power,*
lordship in the NT: one who possesses dominion
Hebrew. *"adon",* *means* **one possessed of absolute control.**
It denotes a master, as of slaves (*Gen. 24:14, 27*), or a ruler of
his subjects.
Heb. seren, applied exclusively to the "lords of a people.
Under a kingly government. (*Jos 13:3 1Sa 6:18*)

In summary a "**Lord**" is the master, the supreme ruler.
The Lord has the control of.
His servants **belong** to him. He has the **power of deciding**, he
possesses and exercises dominion over his subjects.
The Lord rules!
The Lord is "**Lord of**", those that _allow_ him to be their Lord,
or those who gives the Lord, "lordship" by serving the Lord
and obeying the Lord's commands
The Lord is saluted as "Lord".
To belong to a Lord or that a Lord has "Lordship" means
"that the Lord has the government of, or control over,
the person the Lord is Lord of.
The servant is subject to his Lord's *"kingly government"*
THE LORD IS IN CONTROL; NOT THE SERVANT.
Servants **serve** their Lord by **obeying** their Lord rule.
When Jesus Christ is your Lord, he has supreme authority,
dominion and power over you.
You *belong* to the Lord. Body, Soul, and Spirit.

> *For whether we live, we live unto the Lord;*
> *and whether we die, we die unto the Lord:*
> *whether we live therefore, or die, we are the Lord's. Ro 14:8*

When you *give* Jesus Christ "lordship", you give him
the right and authority to Lord over or control you!!
You are "*out of control*", Jesus Christ is "*in control*".
You don't make the decisions for your life anymore,
your Lord does.
Lordship is trusting and obeying the decisions of your Lord,
regardless of how you feel or what you think about it.
You not only *acknowledge* Jesus Christ as Lord,
you are willing for him to *be* lord over you.
You praise and celebrate his Lordship *daily,* not just on Sunday.

ೞ *Lordship* ೞ

"For it is written, [As] I live, saith the Lord,
every knee shall bow to me, and every tongue shall <u>*confess*</u>
to God that Jesus Christ is Lord"
Rom 14:11

The Greek word for "confess" is *"homologeo"*
which means to *"confess, profess, promise, to give thanks*
1) to say the same thing as another, i.e. to agree with, assent
(to agree with God that according to Acts 2:36, JESUS CHRIST IS LORD.)
2) to concede, not to refuse, to promise
(we don't refuse Jesus the right to Lord over us.)
3) to profess to declare openly, speak out freely:
to profess one's self the worshiper of one, to celebrate
If you have any intentions on living permanently in Heaven
after you leave this world, it would behoove you to have
Jesus Christ as your Lord when you get to Heaven.
You can acknowledge and yield to his Lordship now,
or on *that* day.
Either way, one day you *will* acknowledge, and concede to God
that Jesus Christ is Lord!
If you do it now, Our Lord will not say to you...
"I never know you, depart from me ye that work iniquity"
If you do not, you *will* hear,
"I never know you, depart from me ye that work iniquity"
To deny the lordship of Jesus Christ of your life would be to
deny God's Word.

But whosoever shall <u>deny</u> me before men,
him will I also <u>deny</u> before my Father which is in heaven. Mt 10:33
To deny God's kingly government, through the Lordship of
Jesus Christ, in your life, is to expressly deny the will of God.
That he no longer should live the rest of his time in the flesh to the lusts
of men, but to the will of God. 1Pe 4:2

Working in the Church, faithfully attending Church, one's position in the church, one's educational, social or economical successes does not say whether you are saved nor does it guarantee the salvation of your soul.
Doing the will of our Heavenly father will.

And the world passeth away, and the lust thereof: but he that doeth the will of God abideth for ever. 1Jo 2:17

Our Heavenly Father loves obedience to his Word and his will; this is how we are blessed of him.
Rebellion against God's will or his Word will bring dire consequence, no matter how sincere one is.

In flaming fire taking vengeance on them that know not God, and that obey not the gospel of our Lord Jesus Christ:
2Th 1:8
To them who by patient continuance in well doing seek for glory and honour and immortality, eternal life:
But unto them that are contentious, and do not obey the truth, but obey unrighteousness, indignation and wrath,
Rom 2:7-8
If they obey and serve him, they shall spend their days in prosperity, and their years in pleasures.
But if they obey not, they shall perish by the sword, and they shall die without knowledge.
Job 36:11-12

You choose your Lord.
You decide whom you serve.
You, however don't decide the consequences, your actions does.
It's time to know!

Chapter Three

But grow in grace,
and in the knowledge of
our
Lord and Saviour
Jesus Christ.
To him be glory both
now and for ever.
Amen.

2Pe 3:18

Personal Saviour ?

Many Christians have based their salvation on the fact
that they have asked Jesus to "*come into their hearts*"
and that they have "received" or "confessed" Jesus Christ
as their "*personal Saviour*", believing that this is an assurance
of their soul's eternal salvation.
There is no scriptural reference, nor biblical foundation for
either.
It is only a doctrinal and religious belief.
Nowhere in God's word does not tell us to "receive" Jesus
Christ as our "*personal*" Saviour.
Nor does it instruct us to ask Jesus Christ to "*come into our
hearts*".
Our salvation must be based upon the Word of God, not
supposition, man's doctrine or religious beliefs.
Therefore to have accurate knowledge of God's will regarding
our salvation, we must STUDY and search the scriptures
for the truth.
Let's study the scripture traditionally used for these beliefs.
Romans 10:9-11…..which reads as such - .

Rom 10:9 "*That if thou shalt confess* **with thy mouth** **the Lord
Jesus,** *and shalt believe in thine heart that God hath raised him
from the dead, thou shalt be saved.*
Rom 10:10 *For with the heart man believeth unto righteousness
and with the mouth confession is made unto salvation.*"
Rom 10:11 *For the scripture saith, Whosoever believeth on
him shall not be ashamed.*"

To summarize these scriptures -
Rom 10:9 states that *"if "* (*a conditional preposition*)
thou shall "confess"
The definition of confess is - (Greek) *"homologeo" profess,*
promise give thanks, **confession is made**
1) to say the same thing as another, i.e. to agree with, assent
2) to concede 2a) not to refuse, to promise 2b) **not to deny,** *i.e.*
to confess declare 3) to profess i.e. **declare openly,** *speak out*
freely: to profess one's self the worshiper of one 4) to praise,
celebrate
with your mouth... *declare openly with your mouth, to say, to*
confess, to acknowledge **with your mouth** *(not just one time,*
daily) **The Lord Jesus,** *the Lordship of Jesus Christ; that Jesus*
Christ is Lord; that you openly declare that you agree with Acts
2:36 "God made Jesus **both** *Lord and Christ."*
and shall believe *(to think to be true, to be persuaded,)*
in thine heart (*your innermost being, your mind and spirit*)
that God hath raised him from the dead, *(do you really*
believe that God raised Jesus from the dead??)
thou shalt be saved *(safe, made whole and delivered from*
the penalties of the Messianic judgment.)
Nowhere in these scriptures does it instruct us to –
    a) ask Jesus to come into our hearts" (*we must believe in*
    our hearts)
    b) nor does the scripture says to confess him as your
    "personal" Saviour!!" (*The word "Saviour" is not*
    even in these scripture!! It does say to confess
    the Lord Jesus.)
Do you concede that Jesus Christ is Lord?
Do you agree that Jesus was the Christ and is now Lord?

Some don't believe in the resurrection of Jesus Christ from the dead by Jehovah God the Father.

If you do not believe in His resurrection, you can't believe that He is Lord, because he was Lord only *after* his resurrection.

And Jesus came and spake unto them, saying,
power is given unto me in heaven and in earth. Matt 28:18

If, you concede, *if*, you agree that Jesus Christ is Lord, then you must **allow** Jesus Christ to lord over you, or to *be* your Lord.

To acknowledge the Lord Jesus with your mouth means you confess or declare that he is your Lord.

The Scriptures does not tell us to confess him as our Lord just **one** time.

When you give Jesus Christ lordship of your life, you must acknowledge and celebrate him as your Lord daily. You seek his will and accept his government of your life everyday.

You then allow the Lord Jesus to have Lordship (*dominion*) of your life, to lead and guide you according to *his* will.

You obey your Lord, regardless of what your flesh feels, or of what your carnal minds thinks.

In celebrating our Lord, we do not refer to our Lord Jesus as just "Jesus", we would then be robbing Him of His God given deity according to Acts 2:36.

Therefore when we acknowledge (*confess*) Him, we acknowledge him as "our Lord Jesus" every time we refer to, talk about or pray in his name.

For more details on this, please read my new book.
"Declaring the Name of the Lord"
Release date - June 25, 2006.

What is a Saviour, anyway ??

We must now examine the scriptural foundation of what does it mean for the Lord Jesus Christ to be one's "*Saviour*".

I must remind you, again, nowhere in the scriptures does it tell us that Jesus Christ wants to be our "personal" saviour.

Jesus Christ is Saviour of the world!!

And we have seen and do testify that the Father sent the Son to be the Saviour of the world. 1 John 4:14

To dispel this popular myth, we must thoroughly study the word "*Saviour*".

Nelson's Illustrated Bible Dictionary describes "SAVIOUR" A person who rescues others from evil, danger, or destruction. The Old Testament viewed God Himself as the *Saviour*: "There is no other God besides Me, a just God and a *Saviour*" (Is. 45:21).

Because God is the source of salvation, he sends human Saviors (*deliverers*) to rescue His people. (*Ps.106:21*). This word was also used to describe the judges of Israel, those "*Saviours*" or "deliverers" who rescued God's people from oppression by their enemies (Judg. 3:9,15).

In the New Testament the word for "*Saviour*" describes **both** God the Father (1 Tim. 1:1 Jude 25) **and** Jesus Christ the Son (Acts 5:31 Phil. 3:20).

The apostles rejoiced that *in Christ*, **God** had become the "*Saviour* of all men" (1 Tim. 4:10).

He was the Saviour of Gentiles as well as Jews.

The Hebrew meaning for *Saviour* is "*yasha`*" (yaw-shah')

" to be safe causatively, to free or succor: KJV-- avenging, defend, deliver (-er), help, preserve, rescue, be safe, bring (having) salvation, save (-iour), get victory. to be saved (in battle), give victory to.

Israel was God's chosen people. He was a Saviour to
Israel because he "*caused them to be safe*" and freed them
from bondage.

He "*delivered*" them from their enemies, he caused them
to be "*victorious and saved them in battle*",

However God promised a "saviour", a "redeemer" to Israel
that would blot out their perpetual sins.

*Isaiah 59:20 And the Redeemer shall come to Zion, and unto them
that turn from transgression in Jacob, saith the LORD.*

Therefore the "saviour" promised to Israel was Jesus the Christ.
The Greek meaning for "Saviour" is "*soter*" (so-tare') from
the root word "sozo". A deliverer, i.e. God or Christ: - saviour.

> *1) saviour, deliverer, preserver: name was given by the ancients
> to deities, esp. tutelary deities, to princes, kings, etc.*

The word "sozo" means - "safe") *to save, deliver or protect*
KJV-- heal, preserve, save (self), do well, be (make) whole.
In NONE of these scriptures does it instruct us to "receive"
the Lord Jesus as your "personal Saviour"

It is through Jesus the Christ (*the Saviour*) that we obtained
salvation. Salvation is for EVERYONE!

Jesus Christ will not be a Saviour to those who do not believe
in his death or resurrection.

You can, *personally* believe, that Jesus Christ is the Saviour.
You are just acknowledging the fact that Jesus Christ is the
Saviour; but that does not mean that you have given him
Lordship of your life.

Jesus Christ does not want to be your Saviour,
he is already that if you believe in hom.

He wants to be something he may NOT be, - your Lord.

He cannot be your Saviour unless he can be your Lord,
or else the plan of salvation would be ineffective in your life.

He cannot not be one or the other, **he has to be both!**
So therefore, he cannot be your Saviour and not your Lord.

God's word declares Jesus Christ is our Saviour

Luke 2:11 *"For unto you is born this day, in the city of David **a Saviour, which is Christ the Lord.**" (KJV)*
John 4:42 *"And said unto the woman, Now we believe, Not because of thy saying: for we have heard him ourselves, and know that this is indeed **the Christ, the Saviour of the world.**"*
Acts 5:31 *"Him hath God exalted with his right hand to be a Prince and **a Saviour**, for to give repentance to Israel, and forgiveness of sins*
2 Tim 1:10 *"But is now made manifest by the appearing of **our Saviour Jesus Christ**, who hath abolished death, and hath brought life and immortality to light through the gospel:"* (KJV)
Eph 5:23b *".... even as Christ is the head of the church: and he is the **saviour of the body**".* (KJV)
1 John 4:14 *"And we have seen and do testify that the Father sent the Son to be the **Saviour of the world.**"* (KJV)
Acts 13:23 *Of this man's seed hath God according to his promise raised unto Israel **a Saviour, Jesus:** (KJV)*
Phil 3:20 *For our conversation is in heaven from whence also we look for **the Saviour, the Lord Jesus Christ:** (KJV)*
1 Tim 4:10 *For therefore we both labour and suffer reproach, because we trust in the living God, who is the **Saviour of all men,** specially of those that believe. (KJV)*
Matt 1:21 *And she shall bring forth a son, and thou shalt call his name JESUS: for he shall save his people from their sins. (KJV)*
Luke 2:11 *Today in the town of David a **Saviour** has been born to you he is **Christ the Lord.** (NIV)*

Again, we have yet to read *any* scriptures referring to
our Lord Jesus Christ as your "**personal**" Saviour?
As a matter of fact the word "personal" is not even in the
holy Word of God.
It is through the *LORDSHIP* of Jesus Christ that we enter
into the kingdom of Heaven, and inherit the promises of God.
It is *through* <u>**our Lord**</u> Jesus Christ!

> *For the wages of sin is death; but the gift of God is eternal life*
> <u>*through Jesus Christ our Lord.*</u>
> Rom 6:23

> *That the blessing of Abraham might come on the Gentiles* <u>*through Jesus*</u>
> <u>*Christ*</u>*; that we might receive the promise of the Spirit through faith.*
> Gal 3:14

Jesus Christ died for the sins of *all* of mankind.
Everyone has the opportunity to be "*saved, delivered,*
or made whole", but not everyone will.
Acts 2:36 says God made Jesus **both Lord and Christ**.
Notice here the scripture says Jesus Christ is *both*
Lord and Christ (Saviour). **Not one *or* the other**, bur BOTH.
To confess Jesus Christ as your "*personal*" Saviour just
means you "personally" believe that Jesus was the Christ,
and that you personally believe that Jesus Christ paid
the penalty for your sins.
Because you "personally" believe Jesus is the Christ,
does not mean that our Lord Jesus Christ automatically
assumed lordship of your life.
Lordship must be *conceded to, declared openly,* and
yielded to.
It is a cleverly devised trick of Satan for one desiring to be
saved, to just "confess" that Jesus Christ is their "*personal*
Saviour", but do not allow him to be Lord of their life.

Nowhere, in the word of God, does it say that by confessing Jesus Christ as your "*personal Saviour*" it will result in your soul's salvation.

The word "*personal*" means "*individual, familiar, specific*".

While these adjectives may describe a *desired* relationship with our Lord Jesus Christ, it in no way *concedes, declares openly, gives nor yields* lordship to our Lord Jesus Christ! Through a "personal" relationship, our Lord wants you to *know* him, his Word, his will, and his way.

> *Know the Lord: for all shall know me,*
> *from the least to the greatest. Heb 8:1b1*

Without a personal relationship, this will never happen.

To have an abstract knowledge of our Lord (through religion) **does not** *make* him your Lord.

This is why, according to Matt 7:21 our Lord will say to many *"I NEVER KNEW YOU"*

Yes, you may have done many wonderful works in his name, but what about the relationship between you and him?

Were you intimate with your Lord?

Do you *know* him? Does he know *you*?

Do you know his voice? (*My sheep know my voice...John 10*)

You need to become familiar with your Lord.

> "*to grow in Grace and **in the knowledge of***
> ***our Lord and Saviour Jesus Christ*"** *2 Pet 3:18*

Notice it says "grow", which also means to "walk"

> *There is therefore now no condemnation to them which are in Christ*
> *Jesus, who <u>walk not after the flesh, but after the Spirit</u>. Rom 8:1*

It is a process. It will take time. It is not instantaneous.

If you must confess Jesus Christ as your "personal" anything, confess him as "personal" Lord.

He is Saviour of the world. (*John 4:42*)

Chapter Four

No servant
can serve two masters:
for either he will hate the one,
and love the other;
or else
he will hold to the one,
and despise the other.

Lu 16:13

LORDSHIP: A MATTER OF CONTROL!

Control - *to manage, have power over; be in charge of, direct*
We can only have one Lord, and Master.
Because we can only serve one.

> *No man can serve two masters:*
> *for either he will hate the one, and love the other Matt 6:24* ;

A true Lord (*the master*) must have **total** control.
The obedience of a servant to his Lord determines his
relationship with his Lord.

> *"Know ye not, that to whom ye yield yourselves* **servants**
> *to obey,* **his servants ye are** *to whom ye obey , whether of sin*
> *unto death, or of obedience unto righteousness ? Rom 6:16*

A lord's will must be served, because . Lordship commands
obedience
You WILL NOT be neutral in regards to serving your Lord.
You *will* serve whoever lords over you, and you will yield to
that lord's lordship and commands.
The Lord Jesus Christ or Satan, the God of this world. *(2 Cor 4:4)*
Satan wants to deceive you into thinking you can do both,
you cannot.

> *For they that are such serve not our Lord Jesus Christ,*
> *but their own belly; and by good words and fair speeches deceive the*
> *hearts of the simple. Ro 16:18*

That is the trick .....talk holy, look holy, act holy, then
do what you want to do, do what makes you feel good,
have fun, and then just go to church on Sunday,
you got it made Right??? ***WRONG***!!!
As long as Satan can keep you in bondage to the desires
of your flesh and fleshly mind (*to serve them*); he thereby keeps
you under *his* control ***and retains lordship over you.***

Among whom also we all had our conversation in times past in the lusts of our flesh, fulfilling the desires of the flesh and of the mind; and were by nature the children of wrath, even as others.
Ephesians 2:3

If Satan can seduce you into serving your sinful nature, (*your flesh*), and not yield to the Lordship of Jesus Christ, **Satan is still your lord**, not the Lord Jesus Christ.

This I say then, Walk in the Spirit,
and ye shall not fulfill (serve)the lust of the flesh.
For the flesh lusteth against the Spirit, and the Spirit against the flesh:
and these are contrary the one to the other: so that ye cannot do the things that ye would.
Gal 5:16-17

You cannot "walk" in the Spirit (*the Lordship of Jesus Christ*) and walk after your flesh as well.

Because lordship commands obedience, you will **minded** to serve (*obey*) your true Lord, and rebel against any other Lord.

For they that are after the flesh do mind the things of the flesh;
but they that are after the Spirit the things of the Spirit. Rom 8:5

The Lord (whoever it is) will have power over, be in charge of, and direct (*control*) you.

Whomever you serve is your Lord.

Know ye not, that to whom ye yield yourselves servants to obey, his servants ye are to whom ye obey; whether of sin unto death, or of obedience unto righteousness? Rom 6:16 a

If Jesus Christ is your Lord, **his** word, **his** will and **his** way will matter in your life, and that is what you will be minded to walk after.

If Satan is still lord, you will be minded to fulfill the lusts and desires of your flesh.